SOUTHERN CALIFORNIA RAILWAYS

Richard Billingsley

AMBERLEY

First published 2020

Amberley Publishing
The Hill, Stroud
Gloucestershire, GL5 4EP

www.amberley-books.com

Copyright © Richard Billingsley, 2020

The right of Richard Billingsley to be identified
as the Author of this work has been asserted in
accordance with the Copyrights, Designs and
Patents Act 1988.

ISBN 978 1 4456 9631 7 (print)
ISBN 978 1 4456 9632 4 (ebook)

British Library Cataloguing in Publication Data.
A catalogue record for this book is available from
the British Library.

Origination by Amberley Publishing.
Printed in the UK.

Introduction

California, the Golden State, is the Union's largest state by population and the third largest in size. This book will concentrate on the southern half of the state, below an imaginary line from Death Valley, on the Nevada border, to San Luis Obispo, near the Pacific coast.

Of the four main railroads in that area, two provide freight service and own much of the track while two provide passenger service and purchase access to those same tracks.

The Union Pacific Railroad and the Burlington, Northern & Santa Fe Railway, often abbreviated to the BNSF, move many millions of tons of a wide variety of commodities in, through and out of the state annually. The huge ports that line the Pacific coast in the Los Angeles area provide much of that work, with intermodal shipping containers providing a still increasing source of traffic in the form of train after train of containers – many double-stacked to take full advantage of the generous structure heights in the US. There are also plenty of other sites throughout the state which generate traffic of their own. Many large factories and industrial parks still retain a connection to the network and rely on it for deliveries of goods both in and out; there are also many short-line railroad operations which feed traffic to the larger operators' yards.

The BNSF southern trans-continental railroad, the trans-con, leaves the state through the Mojave Desert, to the east, and is one of the most important traffic arteries in the lower 48, linking Los Angeles with Chicago in a similar vein to Route 66; indeed the road was built following the course of the railroad. Upwards of seventy trains are using this crucial track at any given moment – many headed for the BNSF's newly built Intermodal Park near Kansas, MO, which acts as a nationwide hub for container trains.

Both railroads have large classification yards in the state. These receive, sort and dispatch wagon load traffic from all over the country in mixed manifest trains. The BNSF facility at Barstow, in the Mojave Desert, 100 or so miles north-east of Los Angeles, is notable as a large and spacious yard with an almost constant procession of trains in and out. The hump style yard is in use every minute of every day, sorting out individual cars to the correct train. There is also a large diesel shop nearby to provide the locomotives to power the trains.

The National Railroad Passenger Corporation, better known as Amtrak, has an important presence in Southern California, with the frequent and increasingly popular Pacific Surfliner trains plying their trade along the Pacific coast between San Diego, Los Angeles and Santa Barbara. These services are operated by Amtrak California in partnership with Caltrans – the state transport authority – and provide an almost hourly service on the southern section of route, with a handful of services in each direction covering the northern line. The trains use locomotive-hauled double-deck cars, with a cab car on one end to allow easy reversal of the trains. The trains are not especially fast, around three hours is the norm for the 127-mile trip from Los Angeles to San Diego, but they do provide a realistic alternative to the heavily congested I-5 Interstate highway that links the two cities.

Amtrak America operates several long-haul routes into Southern California, including the Coast Starlight from Seattle, the Southwest Chief from Chicago and Sunset Limited from New Orleans; this service also provides through cars from the Texas Eagle service. These trains are but a shadow of themselves during the halcyon years of railroading, but still provide a necessary service to towns and cities along their routes and have become increasingly popular with tourists. With both coach and sleeping accommodation, and on-board catering, the trains are a great way to see the US from the ground.

Commuter rail in the greater Los Angeles area is provided by Metrolink, the Southern California Railroad Authority (SCRRA). Again, using double-deck locomotive-hauled cars, the Metrolink network radiates from Los Angeles Union station to Oceanside (to the south), San Bernardino (to the east) and Oxnard and Lancaster (to the north). Frequent weekday peak-time service is provided, but off-peak and weekend frequency is sparser. Fares are held low to make the service as attractive as possible and trains load well as a result.

Unlike many countries, the US does not have a single railroad track-owning company – the tracks and infrastructure are owned by the individual railroads, who will then sell operating slots to rival owners in a trackage right system. The BNSF and Union Pacific own most of the tracks in Southern California, with the SCRRA owning just a small part extending out from Greater Los Angeles. SCRRA purchased the Antelope Valley route to Lancaster from the Union Pacific, who retain trackage rights as they own the route beyond Lancaster into the Mojave Desert. Amtrak rely entirely on the tracks of others in the area; the only Amtrak-owned rails are on the North East Corridor from Boston to New York and Washington.

In the compilation of this book, I've used photographs taken on around ten visits to the area between 2012 and 2019. The scene is ever changing, and it would be quite impossible to cover the entire area in just one book. The railroads within a 20-mile radius of downtown Los Angeles alone could fill several volumes of this size. The pictures used are intended to show the variety of traffic on offer and the differing locations to be found, from Pacific beaches to the sand and mountains of the Mojave Desert.

All photographs were taken from legally accessible areas and with respect to railroad property. The railroads of America employ their own police forces, who have the same powers to deal with any suspected offence in the same manner as other law enforcement departments, and penalties for trespass can be harsh. The lack of trackside fencing in any area does not make it ok to be on the tracks!

I hope you enjoy viewing the area as much as I have photographing it.

Southern California Locomotive Designations

To the casual viewer, or someone interested in trains who has little knowledge of American railroads, the designations used for differing motive power might seem bewildering. The following notes will help the reader to understand the differing types of locomotives.

For much of the past forty years, the market in the US has been dominated by two manufacturers, Electro-Motive Division (EMD), a General Motors subsidiary until 2005 and now owned by Progress Rail, and General Electric (GE).

The larger of the two manufacturers is General Electric; they currently hold a two-thirds market share. The current Evolution series started production in 2003 and over 5,000 units have been built. Some of the varying types are detailed below.

ES44DC-Evolution Series, 4,400 hp, DC traction motors.
ES44AC-Evolution Series, 4,400 hp, AC traction motors.
ES44C4-Evolution Series, 4,400 hp, AC traction motors, A-1-A trucks with centre unpowered axle.
ET44AC-Tier 4 Evolution, 4,400 hp, AC traction motors.
ET44C4-Tier 4 Evolution, 4,400 hp, AC traction motors.

A letter H at the end of a designation indicates that the locomotive is a ballasted, heavier version with increased tractive adhesion, e.g. ET44AH instead of ET44AC. A CTE designation denotes use of controlled tractive equipment, similar to the Sepex motors used in the UK, e.g. C45ACCTE. The UK Powerhaul Class 70, PH37ACmi is loosely based on the Evolution platform.

Many locomotives built before the Evolution series remain in use. These include the Dash-8 and Dash-9 series locomotives, C40-8W (4,000 hp Dash-8) and C44-9W (4,400 hp Dash-9). Both designs utilise DC traction equipment; these were superseded by the AC4400CW locomotives built with AC motors.

The second manufacturer is Electro-Motive. The company has produced locomotives since the 1930s and became the market leader, overtaking the American Locomotive Company (ALCO) in the 1960s. That dominance was lost to General Electric in the late 1980s. EMD, however, still produces considerable quantities for both domestic and international markets.

The GP (General Purpose) locomotives are four-axle units built from 1949 to 1994 utilising EMD 567, 645 or 710 series engines. Many GPs have been rebuilt for extended service and whilst their days of long-distance, high-speed work are long gone, they are still prolific on local trip workings and yard duty.

The SD (Standard Duty) locomotives are the larger six-axle units built from 1952 onwards using the EMD 265, 567, 645, 710 and 1010 series engines. The SD40 is basically a larger variant of the GP locomotive, but the SD series has evolved to produce large, high powered units such as the SD70ACe, in production since 2003. The Union Pacific is a large EMD customer, over 1,500 of the 4,000 hp SD70M were purchased by the railroad.

The designations on EMD locomotives differ to those on GE locomotives in that the numbering (SD40, SD60 etc.) refer to individual models rather than engine output. SD units up to the SD60M and SD70M used DC motors, the SD60MAC and SD70MAC were the first to offer AC equipment. The SD70MAC was replaced in 2003 by the SD70Ace, which is now the standard EMD heavy-hauler; its latest guise is the SD70ACe-T4 which complies with Tier 4 emissions legislation.

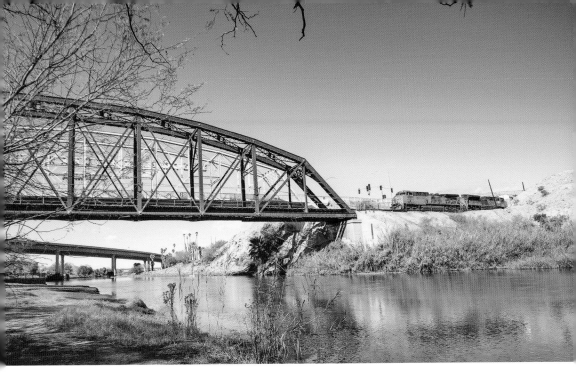

We start in the south-eastern corner of California, as a Union Pacific train of auto-racks crosses the Colorado River from California into Arizona on 5 February 2019. The river forms the border between the two states from here to Fort Mojave, 200 miles to the north.

On the same date, Union Pacific ES44AC No. 8001 emerges into Arizona on the 1923-built Yuma bridge. The coast-to-coast highway bridge alongside unusually predates the railroad bridge and was incorporated into US Highway 80 after its 1915 opening.

As well as bordering each other, Arizona and California both have an international border with Mexico in the Yuma area, and the Mexican influence in the area is strong. This eastbound intermodal train from the Union Pacific Sunset Route is approaching the Yuma bridge and will soon be in Arizona. Seen on 5 February 2019.

A few miles west, at Fort Yuma Reserve, SD70ACe No. 8634 and SD70AH No. 9041 have been held to await the passage over the single-track bridge of oncoming traffic. The late afternoon sun of 3 February 2019 perfectly highlights every detail of these powerful locomotives.

Heading further west, this westbound manifest train, headed by AC4400CW No. 6079, is approaching the Sidewinder Road grade crossing on 3 February 2019. The Sunset Route veers north-west at this point and access to the tracks becomes very difficult, through around 50 miles of uninhabited desert terrain.

Two days later and at the same location, the use of a 250 mm lens gives a completely different view as a Los Angeles bound intermodal train attacks the gradient, with EMD SD70M No. 4956 leading a trio of units. Behind me, the sun is starting to set, giving the late afternoon scene a warm tone.

With the lens dialled back to 175 mm, Sidewinder Road takes on a third perspective. Once again on 3 February 2019, EMD SD70ACe No. 8750 leads a GE unit and a westbound intermodal upgrade away from Yuma. This is the Union Pacific's main route to Texas from the south-west and has dense traffic levels.

Led by EMD SD70ACe No. 8787, more intermodal boxes head west across the All-American canal, at Araz Junction, on 5 February 2019. The man-made waterway takes water from the Colorado River to the Imperial Valley and is also crossed here by a fuel pipeline on the white painted structure.

El Centro lies around 10 miles from the Mexican border city of Calexico; both are served by a quiet branch railway from the main Sunset Route at Niland to Mexicali, just over the border. The storm-laden Saturday afternoon on 2 February 2019 sees two parked GP40s awaiting an inevitable soaking.

On the western end of the border lie both the city and county of San Diego, home to a population in excess of 3 million. The extensive Metropolitan Tram System provides frequent and cheap transportation in the area. An MTS tram arrives into the San Ysidro international border station on 31 January 2019.

The approaches to the Santa Fe depot, home of Amtrak services in San Diego, are cluttered with apartment buildings and low-rise industrial areas. Residents enjoy a grandstand view of Amtrak SC-44 No. 2114 arriving into town with a train from Los Angeles on 1 February 2019. These new locomotives are now in charge of most of the Surfliner services.

The North County Transit District Coaster service provides local trains along the Surfliner route to Oceanside, including to several stations not served by the Amtrak trains. An afternoon view of the Santa Fe depot in downtown San Diego sees EMD F40PHM-2C No. 2105 awaiting homebound commuters, whilst longer distance travellers leave a recently arrived Surfliner from Los Angeles. Taken on 27 June 2012.

As part of the Operation Lifesaver campaign to reduce fatalities at grade crossings, Amtrak California adorned EMD F59PHI No. 457 with this eye-catching livery. Accidents at grade crossings are still an everyday occurrence throughout the country; most are caused by stopped vehicles blocking tracks or drivers ignoring the red lights and barriers.

Two of Coaster's F40PH-2C locomotives stand at San Diego Santa Fe depot on 27 June 2012. These locomotives were purchased in 1995 when the Coaster service commenced and were rebuilds of 1970s F40PH units. Now considered life expired, they are due to be replaced by new Siemens Chargers in 2020.

Locomotive No. 464 is an EMD F59PHI dating from 1998. A fleet of fifteen of these locomotives were the main power for the Pacific Surfliner trains for twenty years. During late 2018 the fleet were replaced by new SC-44 Siemens Charger units. The F59s now belong to Metra – Chicago's commuter rail system.

Coaster also use two F59PHI locomotives alongside their F40PH-2C fleet and one of the pair, No. 3001, arrives into San Diego on the very wet evening of 31 January 2019. Built in 2001, these units may survive in service for a while longer as Coaster wish to increase service provision.

On the same soggy evening, cab car No. 2308 leads a southbound from Oceanside into the Santa Fe at San Diego. These bi-level cars were built by Bombardier in 1994 and allow the train to be driven from the opposite end to the locomotive. This type of operation is extensively used throughout the States.

An early afternoon run from San Diego to Oceanside powers away from the city in the charge of F40PH-2C No. 2102 on 1 February 2019. The journey is around 42 miles in length and takes around an hour. The one-way fare for the ride is currently $6.50.

North County Transit District also provides the Sprinter rail service along the BNSF branch from Oceanside to Escondido. A half-hourly service is provided seven days a week from around 5 a.m. to 9 p.m., and 11 p.m. on Fridays and Saturdays. The terminus at Oceanside allows connections to Amtrak, Coaster and Metrolink services.

With some ideal train-watching balconies behind, Amtrak F59PHI No. 458 arrives at Oceanside Transit Center with a train from Goleta to San Diego. This picture, taken on 1 February 2019, was shot in the last days of the use of these locomotives on the Surfliners, and No. 458 was one of the last to head north to new owners Metra.

Seen at the northern terminus of Coaster services, Oceanside, F40PH-2C No. 2102 is on the rear of a service to San Diego on 1 February 2019. These trains are maintained and stored overnight at Stuart Mesa yard, to the north of the city.

The Sprinter service to Escondido utilises Siemens Desiro VT642 two-car split level diesel multiple units that are maintained in a purpose-built facility close to the Escondido Transit Center. The units generally operate in pairs to provide capacity over the 22-mile route, as seen on this morning service leaving Oceanside on 29 January 2019.

Amid very typical Southern California fauna and flora, Coaster F40PH-2C No. 2102 leads the lunchtime northbound service towards its Oceanside destination on 29 January 2019. Just one set provides the service between morning and evening peak-time, hence you only seem to see one locomotive all day!

The new order on Amtrak's Pacific Surfliners. Replacing the F59PHI locomotives, these 4,400 hp, 125 mph Siemens Charger SC-44s are native Californians, built in state capital Sacramento. Nos 2112 and 2109 pass at Oceanside on 29 January 2019.

The nature of the Pacific Surfliner operation means that it sometimes borrows equipment from other Amtrak service areas. GE Genesis P42DC locomotives have seen frequent use on the route. No. 114 leads a southbound near San Onofre that included a borrowed Superliner car, second from front. Taken on 30 January 2019.

At San Clemente, the tracks meet the shore and trains run alongside the stunning beaches. There is even an Amtrak stop, San Clemente Pier, which is served by Surfliner trains at certain times of the day. Metrolink F59PHI No. 884 pushes south towards Oceanside on 30 January 2019.

The Genesis locomotives have now seen nearly a quarter of a century of Amtrak service. The delivery of new SC-44 units will see at least some of the fleet facing retirement. P42DC No. 151 is standing in for an unavailable SC-44 on a San Diego bound train at San Clemente on 30 January 2019.

Around an hour earlier than the previous picture, SC-44 No. 2114 was caught pushing a Los Angeles bound Surfliner train along San Clemente beach. The train is composed of single-level Horizon fleet cars, with an Amfleet car next to the locomotive. The train is led by a non-powered control unit, converted from an old F40PH locomotive.

The same train moments earlier, showing the ex-F40PH NPCU leading the train. No. 90278 was formerly 1977-built locomotive No. 278. The engine room was gutted, and roller shutter doors were fitted to form a driving car with luggage space. Both pictures were taken from San Clemente Pier.

The All-American Grain Co. at Calipatria has a loop line to load long trains of cars. The train arrives from the north and enters the loop; once the cars have passed through the loader, the train returns to the running line and returns north. Both ends of the train are in view on 6 February 2019.

The town of Niland marks the point where the Union Pacific Sunset Route returns to more viewable terrain. The area is prone to storms rolling in from the Gulf of Mexico and the gathering clouds on the afternoon of 2 February 2019 soon turned to a short burst of torrential rain. Northbound auto-racks leave town behind ES44AC No. 5270.

The engineer of a southbound auto-rack train, headed by GE ES44AC No. 7990, takes a moment away from his cab at Niland as the northbound he has been waiting on passes behind. Cloud and snow cover the caps of the Santa Rosa mountains in the distance, beyond the shores of the Salton Sea. Taken on 6 February 2019.

A few minutes later and No. 7990 is back underway having been given permission to proceed. Niland lies on the 760-mile Sunset Route from Los Angeles to El Paso, TX; this line is one of the most strategically important rail routes in the United States – a quarter of the Union Pacific's traffic originates or terminates in California.

Looking south from the same location a few days earlier, the terrain looks flatter but there is a mountainous area that makes access to photograph the route more difficult. Trying to outrun a gathering storm, GE AC4400CW No. 6455 leads northbound auto-racks over a crossover on 2 February 2019.

A route to Imperial, Calexico, and across the border to Mexicali, leaves the Sunset Route at Niland. This is the line taken by the grain train in picture 30. Los Angeles bound boxes pass the junction to the east of the town, headed by EMD SD70M No. 3888. Taken on 2 February 2019.

Passing at Wister, two intermodal trains each have five locomotives, giving each train around 22,000 hp. Intermodal trains tend to be lighter than other types; usually two or three locomotives will suffice. The green and red unit is a hired-in GE ES44AC owned by Ferrocarril Mexicano – the largest Mexican railroad.

Much of Southern California is geologically active and the area to the east of the Salton Sea abounds with naturally hot springs. This attracts tourists aplenty, and a whole community of businesses such as RV parks and spas serve the area to the east of Highway 111, near to Bombay Beach. A southbound train rattles the billboards on 6 February 2019.

Behind the spa resorts, the Chocolate Mountains form a natural flood divide from the Colorado River. Although not especially high, with a peak around 2,800 ft, the range stands out because the area the photograph is taken in is below sea level. EMD SD70ACe No. 8462 leads a long train of hopper cars north at Pope.

Bombay Beach was a millionaire's playground in the 1950s and 1960s, lying on the shore of the Salton Sea. Sadly, agricultural run-off and natural saline pollution poisoned the sea in the 1970s. This caused a mass extinction of marine life in the salty waters and today the area is virtually abandoned. Taken on 7 February 2019.

A mile or two further along Highway 111, this magnificent reverse curve brings a southbound intermodal making a brisk pace. Almost all the boxes are double-stacked, with over 200 in total aboard. ES44AC No. 7823 leads the entourage on the sultry afternoon of 6 February 2019.

Again, further north on the 111, this marvellous trestle bridge at Ferrum still proudly displays its Southern Pacific heritage, twenty-one years after it was finally swallowed up by the Union Pacific. Union Pacific No. 8384 and Ferromex No. 4016, both EMD SD70ACes, lead a manifest train towards Yuma on 7 February 2019.

A couple of minutes later and the two units on the rear of the manifest train are on the trestle. No. 5577 is a GE AC4400CW, dating from 2004, and No. 7961 is a 2012 Evolution Series ES44AC. The strength of the trestle is proved by the combined weight of just the locomotives, around 370 tons.

The importance of the trestle becomes apparent here: the drainage channel it crosses becomes vital during the flash flood events the area occasionally sees. Without it, the railroad embankment would be in danger of being washed away. A final view from 7 February 2019 with a southbound intermodal passing across.

Heading west into the south of the Greater Los Angeles area and the city of Fullerton is an important stop for both Amtrak and Metrolink services. This picture, from 11 July 2013, was taken during the time that almost every Pacific Surfliner train was powered by the F59PHI locomotives. No. 464 is leaving for San Diego.

Fullerton provides an interchange between the two railroads. This Metrolink EMD F59PH is waiting time with an Orange County Line service to Laguna Miguel on 11 July 2013. These locomotives are now being retired in favour of new EMD F-125 Spirit locomotives.

The palm tree-lined tracks at Fullerton provide a pleasant place to watch trains for an hour or two. Alongside the passenger services, BNSF traffic to and from the Southern Trans-Con runs through the station before heading north-east towards San Bernardino and the Mojave Desert. Taken on 11 July 2013.

Later in the day, Amtrak No. 464 returns north to Los Angeles with its six-car Surfliner train. Fullerton is around twenty-five minutes from Los Angeles Union station by the fastest train. Many choose to live in and around Fullerton because of its easy commute to downtown LA.

And this is the terminal station at Los Angeles Union, pictured on 6 March 2016. The BNSF AC4400CW was one of forty-one units on loan to Metrolink at the time. They were used whilst the company's Hyundai Rotem cab cars were undergoing modifications to prevent obstacles becoming trapped under the front truck in an accident.

Four Rotem cab cars line up at LA Union on 11 July 2013. Taken before problems were detected, the cars had been involved in accidents where they derailed after a collision had occurred. It was determined that the obstacle deflection equipment was not always acting as expected and sometimes allowed debris to lodge under the leading wheels.

A real mixed bag of Amtrak equipment makes up this Surfliner replacement train at LA Union on 11 July 2013. Included is F59PHI No. 451, Genesis P42DC No. 88, a rake of elderly Amfleet single-level cars with a Horizon fleet café car and an ex-F40PH NPCU cab car, providing a driving position at the far end.

Closer inspection of the NPCU No. 90208 reveals its locomotive heritage. EMD F40PH No. 208 was built in 1976. It is one of twenty-three units stripped of their mechanical workings but which retained the ability to control another locomotive from the driving position. The roller-shutter doors aid use of the engine space as checked luggage stowage.

Heading north from LA Union, the first stop is the city of Glendale. The joint Amtrak and Metrolink station is busy throughout the day. This area is home to offices of some big-name entertainment companies. EMD F59PH No. 861 arrives with a train for the Ventura County Line on 18 June 2012.

A tidy looking Amtrak train, powered by EMD F59PHI No. 463, accelerates away from the Glendale call on 26 June 2013. The train is the midday service from Goleta, north of Santa Barbara, to Los Angeles and San Diego. Reversal at LA Union will put the locomotive at the front.

The functional, if somewhat simple, facilities at Glendale station. The platform shelters are very effective at screening passengers from the strong midday sun, but by late afternoon they just provide a place to sit. EMD powered MPI MP36PH-3C No. 892 is on a southbound from the Antelope Valley, next stop LA Union. Taken on 26 June 2013.

Crossing policy can be confusing in some areas. Glendale station has grade crossings for passengers at several points along the platforms, replete with bells and red lights. At Fullerton, a high fence has been installed between the tracks to force people to use the footbridge. Metrolink No. 861 heads north on 26 June 2013.

The next station north is Downtown Burbank. The station and its bus interchange are separated from the downtown area by the I-5 Interstate – a ten-lane freeway through the city. The Ventura County and Antelope Valley lines go their separate ways just north of the station. Taken on 12 July 2013.

Metrolink's oldest F59PH is No. 851, delivered to the railroad in May 1992. Twenty years later, on 19 June 2012, the locomotive powers an airport shuttle to Burbank Bob Hope Airport through Downtown Burbank station. The airport provides limited scheduled services but is an important stop for cargo and private aircraft use.

Burbank is another popular commute; the area is known for being the home of film and TV network studios and many thousands of people rely on the industry for employment. EMD F59PH No. 860 calls to collect homeward bound passengers on 24 June 2013 with an Antelope Valley Line Lancaster service.

Amtrak trains call at the airport station rather than Downtown Burbank. EMD F59PHI No. 459 catches the last rays of 27 June 2012 as it calls with the last northbound train of the day to Goleta. Surfliner service north of Los Angeles is less frequent than the route south – five or six trains per day provide the service.

Metrolink trains to Lancaster take the tortuous former Union Pacific route through Soledad Canyon to climb to the Lancaster plain. The 70-mile Los Angeles to Lancaster trip is around two hours. During the BNSF locomotive hire-in, GE AC4400CW No. 5649 leads a Lancaster to LA Union train on 9 March 2016.

The tracks through the canyon twist and wind their way through desolate scenery as the line climbs from the near sea level Los Angeles to Palmdale, around 2,000 feet up. These tracks now belong to the Southern California Railroad Authority (SCRRA) but the previous owners, Union Pacific, have retained trackage rights along the route.

Bringing up the rear of the train in the previous picture is EMD SD70AH No. 8987. This route from Los Angeles to Mojave is rather shorter than the usual route via the Cajon Pass. Access is limited to slack times in the Metrolink schedule along the route. Taken on 9 March 2016.

With the descent down to Los Angeles about to start, a mid-morning Metrolink service from Lancaster runs through Acton, with EMD F59PH No. 852 pushing a four-car train. The station for the area, Vincent Grade-Acton, is a little further north, close to a Highway 14 exit, and acts as an important park and ride facility. Taken on 9 March 2016.

BNSF AC4400CW No. 5649 is at the rear of a northbound Metrolink train to Lancaster on 9 March 2016 as it crosses the Crown Valley Road near Ravenna, a little to the south of Acton. The locomotive is hooked up to one of the errant Rotem cab cars that were undergoing modification at the time.

Also close to Ravenna, this imposing looking boulder has probably been in the same position for thousands of years, but always looks as if it might let go at any moment. The northbound Union Pacific intermodal hurries by on 9 March 2016.

At the scene of some recent track improvement work, BNSF AC4400CW No. 5641 leads Metrolink train 220 from Lancaster to Los Angeles Union, towards Vincent Grade-Acton station, on 8 March 2016. A policy of continuous improvement is in place for the Antelope Valley Line to reduce journey times down to Los Angeles.

On 1 July 2013, Metrolink No. 881, an EMD F59PHI from 1994, leads train 209 north towards Palmdale. The city of Palmdale lies on the southern section of the San Andreas Fault. At the time of writing, the fault was producing earthquake activity in the Palm Springs area, 100 miles to the south.

After the long climb up through the western end of the San Gabriel Mountains, the Lancaster plain is relatively flat and houses the cities of Palmdale and Lancaster. With the tracks of the Union Pacific route from the Cajon Pass behind the train, Metrolink MPI MP36PH-3C No. 900 sprints between the two cities with train 209 of 8 March 2016.

The tracks return to the Union Pacific north of Metrolink's Lancaster terminal and head north into the Tehachapi mountains. EMD SD70M duo Nos 4393 and 3990 lead a local which seems a little short on custom back towards the small yard at Mojave on 8 March 2016. The location is Rosamund, on the western side of Edwards Air Force Base.

The Union Pacific meets the BNSF route from Barstow at Mojave Junction, with the BNSF utilising trackage rights to Bakersfield. This train has just left Union Pacific tracks. It will now have a relatively easy 70-mile sprint across the Western Mojave Desert to Barstow, before joining the BNSF Southern Trans-Con. Of note is the fifth locomotive, black Illinois Central EMD SD70 No. 1026. Taken on 1 April 2014.

On leaving Mojave, trains face a 2.5 per cent gradient for several miles as they complete the assault of the Tehachapi Mountains. The six locomotives hauling this manifest north from Mojave are a mixed bag, including units from the Canadian Pacific and Norfolk Southern railroads. Taken on 30 March 2014.

With the railroad and Highway 58 running through the town, Mojave is popular with railfans. Overnight accommodation is still relatively cheap, there are plenty of food options and the railroad puts on a show literally yards from the hotel door. BNSF GE C44-9W No. 5170 leads a manifest into town on 24 June 2012.

The long Union Pacific Trona branch heads east from Mojave to an exchange with the Trona Railroad at Searles, around 20 miles from Trona. The former California & Nevada Railroad branch takes traffic to and from North American Salt Mines. A coal train makes progress east near Ceneda on 13 February 2019.

At Searles, the Union Pacific exchanges cars with the Trona Railroad. GE ES44AH No. 8062 has arrived with the coal train from Mojave, which it will now split up and leave in the sidings before taking up the cars on the left to return west. Taken on 13 February 2019.

Despite only being February, the temperatures in the Mojave Desert are up in the mid to high seventies Fahrenheit during the afternoon. The evenings cool rapidly; the heat haze being emitted by these four BNSF units slugging north is testament to how hard this climb is. Taken on 11 February 2019.

The small yard at Mojave handles traffic to and from the Lehigh Cement Plant at Monolith, near Tehachapi. The local is seen at Warren, returning down to Mojave, on 31 March 2013. It is led by two EMD SD60Ms – Nos 2384 and 2437.

Night is rapidly falling over the Mojave as the 'earthworm' grain train heads up from Mojave on 15 September 2018. So-called because the individual brown cars look like the segments of a worm from afar, this massive train can exceed 150 loaded cars and utilises nine locomotives – four in front, three mid-train and two at the rear.

The same spot in the bright afternoon sun of 6 April 2014. BNSF GE ES44C4 No. 6563 leads a northbound JB Hunt intermodal upgrade. Note the telegraph pole line on the right of the train, disused and falling into disrepair. The railroad had removed all trace of it in the previous picture from 2018.

The private railroad crossing at Warren, with a train of autoracks approaching. It is the policy of most railroads to close grade crossings where possible; their misuse is the single highest cause of accidents on the tracks. The closure notice was captured on 30 June 2013; this crossing was still open in February 2019.

The area around Warren, a couple of miles north of Mojave, is also popular with railfans – long swooping curves with trains being worked hard over gradients will always attract attention. Two BNSF manifest trains, both with red and silver Santa Fe Warbonnet liveried locomotives, pass on 1 April 2014.

Another factor in the area's popularity is the wide variety of locomotives that find their way to the area. This BNSF manifest has power from the Norfolk Southern and Canadian Pacific as well as the BNSF themselves. An average day in the area will usually feature locomotives from four or five of the eight class one railroads.

Always expect the unexpected. This long line of BNSF power features Santa Fe 2229, an elderly EMD GP38. You wouldn't normally expect to see this type of locomotive in the area, but transfers between operating areas or shop visits are catered for by adding the units to trains that are already running, rather than by special movement. Taken on 4 July 2013.

Light and shade on Union Pacific EMD SD70ACe No. 8369 at Warren on 11 February 2019. The locomotive is at the rear of the train, the formation making an abrupt turn to the west up ahead before making the final assault of Tehachapi summit.

As will be seen in the next few pictures, there are thousands of wind turbines on the higher slopes of the Tehachapi Mountains, where strong desert winds occur throughout the year. Running adjacent to Highway 58, this late afternoon Union Pacific intermodal is at Cameron Road on 15 September 2018.

Springtime in Tehachapi can produce all four seasons in one week, and 2 April 2014 was winter. Despite the location being on the edge of a desert, winter snow is not a rarity, but it was certainly unusual in April. This is just a sprinkling; a bad winter will see in excess of 12 inches of fallen snow.

Just four days later and the outlook is completely different, as BNSF 6563, a GE ES44C4, takes a train of intermodal boxes towards Tehachapi. The location is Eric. At this point the tracks dive under Highway 58 and veer around a dry lake before running alongside the cement plant at Monolith.

Climbing towards Eric in a snowstorm on 30 March 2014. Poor rail adhesion can be a problem during bad weather, and it isn't unknown for trains to slip to a stand on the gradients in the Tehachapi Mountains.

GE AC4400CW No. 5564 leads a four-locomotive manifest train past the cement works at Monolith on 29 June 2013. An important local employer and source of railroad traffic, the works opened in 1908 providing materials for the construction of the LA aqueduct – a waterway to take water down to Los Angeles from the Owens River.

30 March 2014 sees Union Pacific EMD SD70ACe No. 8802 taking late afternoon intermodal boxes north at Monolith. The days are short in winter: it's only a little past five in the evening and already the sun has dipped behind the mountains to the west.

If on time, the late afternoon to early evening pass of the northbound BNSF 'earthworm' grain train can produce some interesting low light results. This picture from 9 March 2016 shows GE ES44C4 No. 6542, at the head of the train, passing Monolith at around 5.45 p.m.

Tehachapi summit in fine weather on 2 March 2016. At just under 4,000 feet, the summit is a bit of respite for both train and crew. That relief is short lived, however: controlling 10,000+ tons of train down a 2.5 per cent gradient is just as difficult as getting them up in the first place.

The section of track between Tehachapi and Bakersfield consists of over twenty miles of twisting track, more akin to roller coaster than railroad, before an almost straight run into Bakersfield and the San Joaquin Valley. Union Pacific boxes heading up to Tehachapi past Marcel on 2 July 2013.

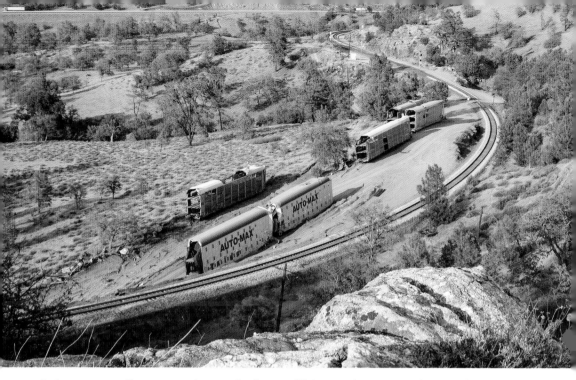

And sometimes it all goes wrong. A rear end collision at Walong involving a stopped intermodal and a train of auto-racks during May 2013 stopped traffic for two days. On 29 June 2013, some of the wrecked racks were still awaiting removal.

A few minutes after the previous picture, a Union Pacific manifest train passes the collision site. You can appreciate the reason why some of the wreckage remains on site some weeks after the accident from this picture – the terrain makes removal rather difficult.

The world-famous Tehachapi loop is at Walong, a few miles north of Tehachapi itself. In barely a mile of track, trains loop over themselves and climb, or descend, 77 feet of elevation. This southbound is on the outer part of the spiral. Sadly, viewing the spectacle becomes more difficult each year due to tree growth.

The line curves past the town of Keene – a town that once relied on the Union Pacific for water supplies. Looking south from Keene with an approaching BNSF intermodal on 6 July 2013, GE Dash-9 No. 4357 leads the four units powering the train.

The gradient through Keene becomes more apparent looking to the north. Another BNSF four-unit intermodal disturbs the peace as it hammers upgrade on 3 March 2016.

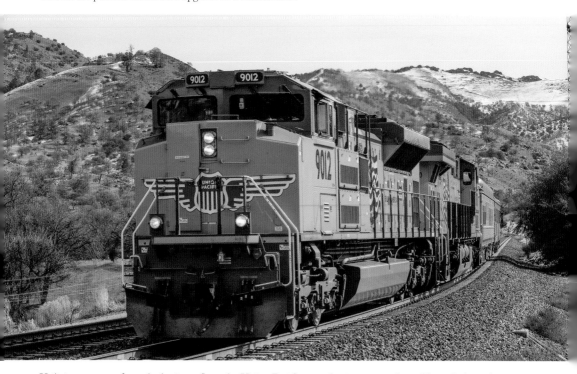

Utilising two cars from the heritage fleet, the Union Pacific ran a business special northbound along the route on 12 February 2019. A very clean EMD SD70AH-T4C No. 9012 leads at Keene. Note the camera in the right-side window, a standard fitting in locomotives today.

Union Pacific equipment at Bealville, 7 March 2016. The area was named for Edward Fitzgerald Beale, a district superintendent and landowner in the area. His ranch, Rancho El Tejon, is still in existence today.

Looking across the ranch from Bealville grade crossing, the line south can be viewed on the hillside as trains emerge from Tunnel 3, far right. Tunnel 4 was also in view from here until it was destroyed by the earthquake of 1952. Pictured on 22 June 2012.

Trackside space and a siding at Bealville are often used to assist with maintenance of way operations in the area – Bealville Road allows easy access for trucks from Highway 58. A southbound intermodal passes plant stationed in the area on 1 March 2016.

The unlucky SUV driver has a moment or two to wait as BNSF No. 7162 leads north across Bealville grade crossing on 2 April 2014. It could be worse: a long train here would be visible at Tunnel 3, above the dark blue containers.

The two-car business special (seen earlier) from 12 February 2019 rounds the curve exiting Tunnel 2 above Caliente. The railroad passes through the town on a long horseshoe curve before regaining its northbound path towards Bakersfield.

Caliente is where the terrain changes as the San Joaquin Valley gives way to the foothills of the Tehachapi Mountains. The railroad's steep course south away from the town is only too evident in this scene from 1 April 2014. Note the hired-in Citirail ES44AC, second in formation.

The end of mountainous terrain is in sight for the BNSF train dropping down into town. For the Union Pacific manifest in front, the real work is about to begin. Taken in Caliente, 17 September 2018.

This southbound BNSF train has just negotiated the Caliente horseshoe curve and has now started the ascent towards Tunnel 2. Seen on 2 April 2014, the relatively green countryside will be entirely yellow by June as 100 plus degree Fahrenheit temperatures take hold.

The business train passes over the flowing waters of Caliente Creek on 12 February 2019. The two cars, *Stanford* and *Sunset*, are old UP passenger cars from 1927 and 1955 and have been modernised to provide full living accommodation for their lucky riders – the high-end management.

Looking north along Bena Road from virtually the same location. Bena Road becomes Edison Road and leads to Bakersfield; the railroad stays close by virtually all the way to town. Once at Kern Junction, the BNSF splits away and takes a more westerly path to the San Francisco. Taken on 1 March 2016.

We're at Bena on the southern tip of the San Joaquin Valley now – a fertile area for growing, albeit with modern piped irrigation. It doesn't rain so much, but when it does rain, you're going to get very wet. 11 March 2016 was notably so; this southbound was caught from inside the car.

Bena in the sun. The hot Saturday afternoon of 23 June 2012 saw a southbound UP intermodal, led by SD70M No. 4453, entering the single-track section that will take it through the creek to Caliente. Behind the train is the double-track section to Bakersfield.

Bena on 12 February 2019. A BNSF southbound waits to access the single track ahead. The telegraph pole line referred to on page 46 is still in existence here. Its disuse is evident: notice the broken wires that hang down in the foreground.

With very little to block the setting sun before it dips below the horizon, the area from Bena, through Edison to Bakersfield, is ideal for a golden hour shot if conditions and clouds permit. With one of the four units clearly needing a shop visit, this BNSF manifest arrived at the perfect time on 28 February 2016.

Bena attracts the photographer's attention for other reasons too. Trains are sometimes held here to allow more important traffic to pass and crew changes are sometimes performed here, rather than blocking tracks in Bakersfield. The BNSF train here has been held whilst a small air leak is attended to. The Union Pacific passes on the other track. Taken on 28 February 2016.

Another long, hot California summer has taken its toll on the landscape. The yellow grass suggests it's been some months since any significant rain. Trains of piggyback semi-trailers are a common sight at Bena. This BNSF northbound was led by GE ES44C4 No. 6556 on 17 September 2018.

The last view of Bena is from up high, from a local route that leads to the Kern County Municipal Waste Center. It's early March 2016 as a Union Pacific manifest leaves the mountains behind on what was a distinctly cool day for the area, with temperatures barely reaching the 60s.

Sandcut had a Southern Pacific cantilever signal bridge like that at Tehachapi. Both were replaced when the Union Pacific re-signalled the tracks over the mountains. The replacement equipment lies in wait alongside the old equipment on 5 July 2013.

We're arriving into the southern reaches of the city of Bakersfield now as a UP train crosses Weedpatch Highway. Alongside is the Bakersfield Power Company installation, now operated by So Cal Edison. Taken on 2 April 2014.

The Union Pacific diesel yard at Bakersfield had a turntable (to the left) and fuelling lines (right). It dated from Southern Pacific days when extra locomotives would be attached for the mountainous trek to Tehachapi. Closed just a few months later, this view is from 2 July 2013.

Seen in the sidings, alongside the old Southern Pacific depot in Bakersfield, on 23 June 2012, is locomotive No. 280, an EMD GP38-2 locomotive dating from 1980. The locomotive was Missouri Pacific No. 2166 when new, passing to the UP in the 1982 takeover of the MP.

The new Amtrak station opened on 4 July 2000 and is situated a little to the south of the old station, on the BNSF tracks to the north. The station is the southern terminus of the San Joaquin service, running seven times daily to either Oakland or Sacramento. GE Genesis P42DC No. 136 waits with train 717, the 2.12 p.m. to Oakland, on 3 March 2016.

The San Joaquin services are similar to the Pacific Surfliners, using bi-level passenger cars with a cab car on the opposite end to the locomotive. The trains had dedicated F59PHI units at the time, but in theory any Amtrak locomotive can be used. GE Genesis P42DC No. 116 powers away from Bakersfield on 8 April 2014.

Savage Services Corporation has a facility in Wasco, north of Bakersfield, and utilises its link to the BNSF railroad. The locomotive, No. 8611, is an EMD GP7u, dating from October 1952, new to the Atcheson, Topeka & Santa Fe Railroad. Taken on 8 April 2014.

Classic railroad colours on display alongside California Highway 43 at Shafter, near Wasco. The two Warbonnet-liveried locomotives are Nos 141 and 119, both EMD GP60Ms dating from 1990. The 1998 merger of the ATSF and Burlington Northern railroads made this livery obsolete. Taken on 8 April 2014.

Alongside milepost 913, Wasco Amtrak is the first stop north of the San Joaquins. GE Genesis No. 98 takes train No. 712 from Oakland to its destination, Bakersfield, on 8 April 2014.

Trackside at Wasco station, 8 April 2014. To celebrate its fortieth anniversary in 2011, Amtrak painted several Genesis units in heritage paint schemes. Locomotive No. 156 carries the phase 1 livery, introduced in 1972. This livery was nicknamed 'bloody nose' by railfans for obvious reasons.

Back on the Pacific coast and Amtrak 'cabbage car' No. 90208 leads Surfliner 792 from Goleta to San Diego at Dulah on 10 July 2013. The train was due to San Diego at 11.03 p.m., around five and a half hours after the picture.

At just over 100 miles north of Los Angeles, the city of Santa Barbara enjoys a half dozen Surfliners in each direction daily, plus the long-distance Coast Starlight service to Seattle. EMD F59PHI No. 454 arrives into town on 25 June 2013 with train 777 from San Diego to San Luis Obispo – a further 120 miles north.

The two locomotives and twelve cars of the southbound Coast Starlight arrive into Santa Barbara on 25 June 2013. The thirty-five hour, 1,377-mile itinerary of train 11 starts in Seattle, WA, passing through Portland and Eugene, OR, then through California via Sacramento, Oakland, San Jose and Santa Barbara before reaching Los Angeles.

Our time in the desert begins at Victorville, a city currently famous for storage of grounded Boeing 737 Max aircraft. The city lies on the BNSF tracks that form the railroad's main approach to the Los Angeles area from the Southern Trans-Con. GE ES44C4 No. 6513 brings empty cars through on 3 April 2014.

To the north of Victorville, the TXI-Riverside cement plant at Oro Grande provides work for these two EMD GP40s owned by Harbor Rail Services. Seen on 3 April 2014, the pair were still resident in late 2017. Locomotive leasing is big business in the US, but units are often exchanged for others for maintenance purposes.

The Boron local takes traffic from Barstow yard destined for the US Borax mine at Boron. The train runs most days and is generally a good opportunity to see some smaller and older BNSF units out on a main line. An all EMD line-up was viewed at Boron on 29 February 2016; the Burlington Northern green GP39-2 dates from 1964.

Some days, something newer and bigger will lead the train. On 9 April 2014 GE C44-9W No. 4132 is seen taking the return train over the Twenty Mule Team Road grade crossing in Boron. The Dash 9 was very likely on a test run after maintenance in Barstow diesel shop.

The line to Boron mine joins the BNSF Mojave sub, a 70-mile dash across the desert between Barstow yard and the Union Pacific tracks at Mojave. BNSF traffic from the Southern Trans-Con uses this route, via the UP tracks, to access northern California. ES44C4 No. 8349 makes fast progress east on 4 March 2016.

Unusually in this age, the Boron local requires the use of a caboose on the spur to the mine. This is kept on the spur beside the main tracks when not in use. In July 2013 a heavily graffitied ex-ATSF car, No. 999798, was in use and is seen parked at Boron awaiting the next train.

The San Gabriel Mountains form a formidable natural barrier between populous Los Angeles and the desert wilderness – trains go over the mountains via the Cajon Pass. This BNSF northbound is nearing the summit at Cajon Junction on 4 April 2014.

We reach Barstow, a major point in railroading terms. On the western end of the Trans-Con, the city's classification yard splits traffic for northern and southern California and provides crews and locomotives. This train, joining the Mojave sub west, includes units from Kansas City Southern and Citirail and an ex-Santa Fe GP60. Taken on 4 April 2014.

Empty spine cars pass Barstow Amtrak on 7 April 2014. Locomotive No. 8090 leads, a GE ES44C4 that had only been in service for a couple of weeks at the time. Behind is No. 4078, a GE C44-9W from 2003. The new Evolution series locomotive owes much to the success of its Dash-9 predecessor.

At Nebo, a few miles east of Barstow, Route 66 joins the tracks of the Trans-Con for the journey east; they will be side by side for much of the 140 or so miles to Needles, close to the Arizona border. The BNSF rolls downgrade from Daggett towards Barstow on 10 March 2016.

The Union Pacific utilises BNSF tracks from Cajon to Daggett, via Barstow, before turning off onto their own route north, through Las Vegas and onto Salt Lake City. With all units under power, four GE and three EMD locomotives will soon be slowing for the 15 mph junction at Daggett and its abrupt left turn. Taken on 31 January 2017.

Headlights blazing, this BNSF train is heading out into the desert for an overnight run east. The setting sun and the direction of the tracks work perfectly for 'golden hour' shots here at Daggett, the added bonus being that cloudy evenings are a rarity here. Taken on 4 April 2014.

Union Pacific stacks 'n' racks at Daggett on 18 September 2018. The train will stop at the yard in Yermo, a couple of miles to the north, to change crew before continuing north. GE ES44AC No. 7788 leads the formation towards the junction.

Yermo has a very large US Marine Corps base. The US armed forces are a large railroad user for the movement of equipment. This train had just left the base and was caught at Daggett on 11 February 2019. Southern Pacific 'Patch' AC4400CW No. 6379 leads a CSX ES44AH, No. 3166. There are now only a handful of SP liveried units left.

After the crew change, the stacks 'n' racks train from page 78 makes a rapid departure from the UP Yermo yard. The train will see little in the way of human activity for the next 115 miles north before the barren desert gives way to the bright lights and buildings of Las Vegas.

Looking north from the same spot, a manifest creeps south past an intermodal, stopped for a crew change, on 11 February 2019. The relief crew will have been brought up from the yard by the silver minivan – this will also return the relieved crew to the depot to book off duty.

Approaching Yermo from the north, this intermodal has been stopped to await its place in the traffic at Daggett. The locomotive is a short distance from the controlling signal but has stopped short to avoid blocking Minneola Road grade crossing. Taken on 19 September 2018.

A view of the Cool Water generating plant from Route 66 on 31 January 2017. A passing BNSF intermodal runs west; the two locomotives are at the rear of the train. Behind the plant can be seen some of the buildings that make up the USMC base at Yermo.

A 3-mile drive along Minneola Road from the UP tracks will bring you to the BNSF grade crossing on the Trans-Con. GE ES44C4 No. 6918 and three more, including hired-in CSX traction, bustle westwards on 19 September 2018.

With one unit clearly in need of a visit to the diesel shops, a westbound manifest train restarts from a signal stop on the Trans-Con at Minneola Road on 7 April 2014. On arrival at Barstow, the locomotives detached and left in the direction of the shop, which is situated at the south end of the yard.

Four units, unusually running nose to tail 'elephant style', take a domestic intermodal east at Minneola on 31 January 2017. This type of train provides the modern image the railroads wish to present of long, fully loaded trains at speed. Note the Norfolk Southern unit in position four.

Approaching Newberry Springs, Route 66 and railroad briefly separate before re-joining, albeit with the I-40 Interstate to separate them. On 7 April 2014, this intermodal gingerly passes two technicians working on a faulty switch on the track the train is using.

For the twenty-five or so miles east from Newberry Springs to Ludlow, the railroad, Interstate I-40 and Route 66 are in close proximity, all following the same mountain passes. The I-40 veers away at Ludlow and won't be seen until Essex, over sixty miles east. GE ES44DC No. 7473 climbs away from Ludlow on 10 March 2016.

Heading in the opposite direction, GE ES44C4 No. 8328 passes the same location an hour or so after the previous photograph was taken. 100 Fahrenheit temperatures are common here and, if following Route 66 and the railroad, Ludlow is the last place you'll be able to buy a cold drink until you reach Amboy, forty miles distant.

The GE Evolution series locomotives and their predecessors are standard fare for the BNSF in the Mojave Desert, the railroad preferring to use its EMD high-powered units on heavy coal workings. The sight of a SD70ACe at Ludlow is not by any measure unique; unusual is perhaps a better description. 10 March 2016 saw this unit head west on a train of empties.

The Barstow to Cadiz local takes cars to the Arizona & California Railroad, at Cadiz, for onward shipment by the ACR to Parker. The train is always one to look out for as it usually employs some of Barstow's smaller and older units. 18 September 2018 didn't disappoint as five EMD GP60/GP60M locomotives power back to Barstow with the return.

Trains heading east and west cross near Ash Hill on 7 February 2014. Locomotives carrying the long-obsolete silver and red Warbonnet livery are evident on both trains – a sight that becomes rarer each passing year as units are re-painted or retired.

Siberia, San Bernardino County, 10 March 2016. The run through the desert along the 66 is a fantastic place to watch and photograph the trains. The quiet highway provides a huge choice of places to stop and the frequency of traffic will mean you don't have time to get bored. All you need to be aware of is sunburn and the snakes…

The next few photographs show the banked curves at Siberia. The two tracks separate for a while and westbound trains climb away from those headed east. GE ES44C4 No. 8124 takes an eastbound around the lower track on 18 September 2018.

With the help of sun and shadow, this westbound makes an imposing sight as it takes the higher-level track around the curve on 10 March 2016. The curvature of the tracks and the change in elevation are clearly apparent; the train will head north for a mile or so before returning to its westbound course.

Seen earlier at Ludlow, the locomotives on the Cadiz local on 10 March 2016 attack the curves. The units date from 1989 to 1991 and show how locomotive design changed around that time. EMD's latest SD70 design has the same 'teardrop' window cab design as that of GP60M No. 144, the lead unit.

The Trans-Con through the desert is signalled bi-directionally, this allows flexibility in day-to-day operation. With no eastbound traffic in the area, this westbound intermodal has switched tracks to pass a slower moving manifest service. No. 3851, a Tier 4 GE ES44C4, leads on 30 January 2017.

A trio of GE Dash-9s head west on 7 April 2014. Lead locomotive No. 4706 was part of a batch of locomotives that were completed around the time of the Burlington Northern and ATSF merger was announced; they were left in Santa Fe colours but given BNSF branding. The loco was still carrying the colours in September 2019.

You'd be forgiven for thinking this is a summer scene; it was shot on 9 February 2019 as a train takes the higher track west. With temperatures at around 75 Fahrenheit, it was slightly warmer than normal for the time of year, but rather more pleasant than the 100 degrees you'd expect in July.

BNSF Dash-9 No. 4073 and ES44C4 No. 6827 at East Siberia on 9 February 2019. The bridge looks as if it has little purpose, but its role is vital in the monsoon type weather seen in the fall of some years. Over fifty similar bridges of wooden construction on Route 66 were badly damaged in the flash floods of 2014.

Taken from the tarmac of Route 66, this westbound is making steady progress near Bagdad on 4 March 2016. It is possible to pick up on a train and photograph it in several locations; the proximity of tracks and highway and the relatively low speed of the trains allow a picture around every two to three miles without breaking any speed limits!

Sadly, the geographic location of the Mojave Desert doesn't allow for a long, hot evening of photography. This shot, taken at 5.21 p.m. Pacific time on 9 February 2019 at Bagdad, between Siberia and Amboy, is catching the last glimpse of daylight. Even in the summer, the sun has gone by just after 7 p.m.

With typical desert scenery of mountains and scrubland, BNSF GE ES44C4 No. 6911 and borrowed Norfolk Southern GE D9-40CW No. 9964 are panned as they pass Bagdad with a train of empty well cars on the same day, but around ninety minutes earlier.

With the world-famous Roy's Motel and gas stop at Amboy visible in the backdrop, this shot shows the area around Amboy crater from up high on a mound of solidified black volcanic rock. The relatively easy climb allows you to see for about five miles to the west and fifteen miles east, making it easy to see trains approaching. Taken on 10 February 2019.

The Cadiz eastbound local approaches Amboy on 10 March 2016. The motive power, as ever, is interesting as it contains older Dash-8 locomotives in four different liveries, including original Santa Fe Warbonnet units in positions two and three. Leading unit No. 516 is rebuilt and carries the latest BNSF Heritage 4 scheme.

Despite the blue skies, the sun is obscured as two Dash-9s sandwich an EMD SD70M near Amboy on 7 April 2014. The SD70M was almost the standard Union Pacific locomotive for some years; the fleet numbers around 1,500 units. The BNSF preferred the Dash-9, and still runs nearly 1,600 of the type.

Featuring five EMD GP60 or GP60M locomotives, the westbound Cadiz local takes power approaching the grade crossing at Amboy on 18 September 2018. Picking the train up here, it was possible to take pictures of it at several locations between here and Ludlow, more than thirty miles west.

30 January 2017 sees Union Pacific No. 7700, a GE Evolution series ES44AC, leading two more locomotives and a good length of double-stack intermodal boxes. The train is running eastbound through Cadiz, a dozen or so miles to the east of Amboy. The second unit is a CSX GE Evolution.

Just before 5 p.m. on 10 February 2019 and the Cadiz local arrives at its destination. The remote desert location has storage sidings and an exchange with the Arizona & California Railroad – a shortline that meanders 190 miles south-east through the Mojave to Parker, AZ, and a junction to the BNSF at Matthie, AZ.

A mile or so beyond Cadiz, a long sweeping curve takes the Trans-Con in a more north-easterly direction as the line heads away towards Needles and the Arizona border. The curve stretches out a westbound on 30 January 2017, showing just how long these trains can reach.

A view of the Cadiz local, seen on page 94, as it rounds the curve onto Arizona & California Railroad tracks. The five BNSF units will leave the complete train on the curve, then go to the exchange sidings to collect the return cars from the ACRR before returning to Barstow.

Another westbound bears down on Cadiz, this time on 8 February 2019. Despite over four years having passed since the flash flooding of the 2014 fall, the area around Cadiz still bears many scars from the event; most of the wood in the picture was carried here by floodwaters.

Much of the line east from Cadiz to Needles is visible, but not accessible from Route 66. Railroad and highway follow the same course but are often separated by four miles of rough desert terrain. With the Arizona border in sight, a train starts out over the Colorado bridge at Topock on 29 January 2017.

The rough terrain between the Moabi Regional Park and the bank of the Colorado River has an almost lunar-like landscape, on 10 April 2014, as GE ES44DC No. 7518 heads east towards darkening night skies. The park lies behind the train and offers a wide variety of water-based recreational activity.

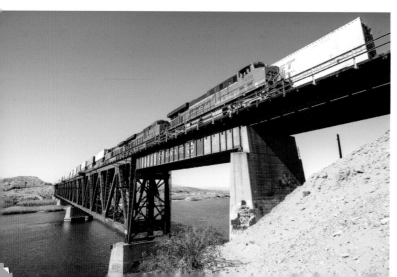

We end our tour of the southern half of the Golden State as we began – crossing the Colorado River on steel girders crossing blue waters. Topock, AZ, welcomes GE ES44DC No. 7470 as it enters the Grand Canyon State on 29 January 2017.